Ready Steady Sing!

songs with musical activities for 3-7 year olds

(Key Stage 1)

Jane Sebba

Music and text © 1994 by Jane Sebba
First published in 1994 by Faber Music Ltd
3 Queen Square London WC1N 3AU
Cover illustration by Kelly Dooley
Music and text processed by Seton Music Graphics Ltd
Printed in England by Halstan & Co Ltd
ISBN 0 571 51497 9

FABER *ff* MUSIC

6-95

Preface

All the songs in this book have been tried and tested in the classroom. The songs are written to suit an age range of three to seven, but I've used many of them with eight, nine and ten year olds. They are designed to be adaptable and can be altered to meet your requirements regarding class size, space, available instruments, etc. The activities with each song are intended only as a guide, and my real intention is that the songs are moulded by you and your children as you use them. The companion book *Strike up the Band!* (Key Stage 2) also contains many songs suitable for use at Key Stage 1 level.

Using the songs

* Many of our sessions take place with everyone, including the teacher, sitting on the floor in a circle, and we often sing songs unaccompanied, especially when introducing new material.

* Use plenty of body percussion (making percussive sounds using just the body, e.g. clapping, stamping, etc.) before introducing instruments, to enable the children to feel the rhythms before having the added responsibility of managing an instrument.

* Where it's appropriate, end songs with a verse for everyone to join in (e.g. 'Isn't it grand to play in the band on the instruments . . .').

* Try starting and ending each song with a game of musical statues – valuable early training for performance.

* Encourage the children to think of new verses wherever appropriate. Personalised songs work well, and are fun.

* Use the versatility of the songs to stretch the children at whatever stage they may be. For instance, *While you sing this song* (p.38) can incorporate all *these* ideas and thousands more:

Take giant steps while you sing this song
Clap your hands while you sing this song
Sway to the beat . . .
Play the tambourine . . .
Make a crescendo . . .
Play a dotted rhythm . . .
Play slow beats . . .

* Where only one line or word is changed in each verse, this has been highlighted by using italics.

* The ♩ ♩ notes above some songs indicate rhythms for actions within the song, i.e. clapping, clicking, stamping feet, percussion sounds, etc.

* The guitar chords are not always exactly the same as in the piano accompaniment. More manageable alternatives to difficult chords are included.

* The 'Learning Labels' given with each song are linked to educational activities included in the National Curriculum (Music Key Stage 1 – you will also find that many of the songs are suitable for use at Key Stage 2 and pre-school level).

* For convenience, children are referred to as either 'him' or 'her'.

* Throughout the book the figure ♪♫ is not to be taken literally, but as the jazz convention for ♪♪.

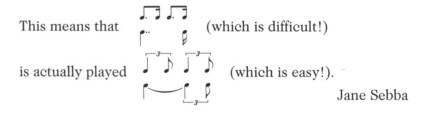

This means that (which is difficult!)

is actually played (which is easy!).

Jane Sebba

Contents

for Dot Fraser and Tamar Swade,
who have sung these and many other songs with unfailing good cheer

Acknowledgements

For ideas and opinions, my thanks to Dot Fraser, Vivien Lewis, Tamar Swade and Allan Watson.

6-95

We're ready

Two claps, two stamps, then any other action of your choice.

1. We're ready to clap our hands,
   And we're ready to stamp our feet,
   So it's ready steady go to tap our heads
   And we'll do it to a steady beat.

2. We're ready to clap our hands,
   And we're ready to stamp our feet,
   So it's ready steady go to wiggle our bottoms
   And we'll do it to a steady beat.

You will need

Some space.

How it Happens

The claps (bar 4) and stamps (bar 6) remain constant in every verse, but the third action (bars 8, and 11-18) can be changed each time.

Teaching Tips

Encourage smaller children to count 1- 2- aloud as they clap and stamp.

Educational Extras

Add some dynamics to the performance.

Choose one child to be in charge of volume control during bars 11-18. Place her where she can be seen by the rest of the class. Arms wide apart indicate an increase in volume, arms together a decrease.

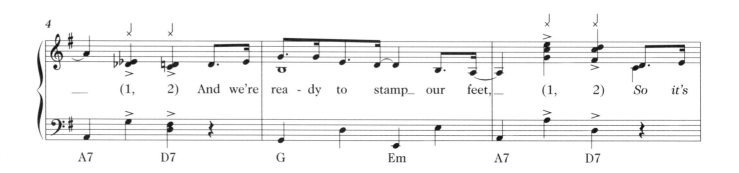

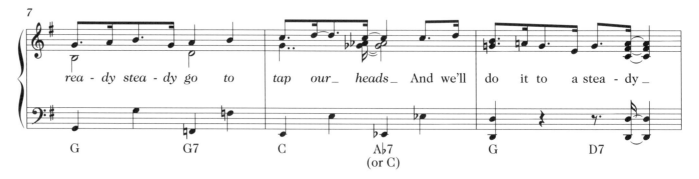

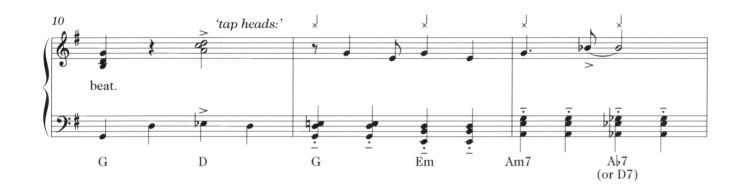

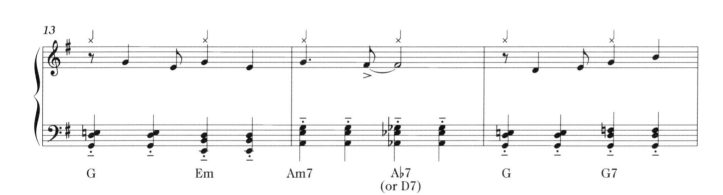

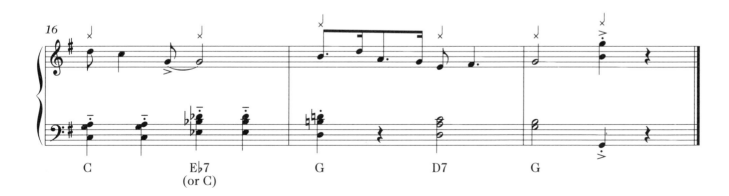

Learning Labels

* singing in unison
* memorising a melody
* learning and repeating simple rhythmic patterns
* choosing and performing actions to a steady beat
* watching and responding to a conductor

1. Hear the music and *nod your head*,
   Hear the music and *nod your head*,
   Hear the music and *nod your head*,
   Till you hear the end and then keep
       still.

2. Hear the music and *knock your knees*,
   Hear the music and *knock your knees*,
   Hear the music and *knock your knees*,
   Till you hear the end and then keep
       still.

You will need

Some space

Any mixture of percussion instruments.

How it Happens

Sing and perform any activity that you or the children choose throughout, but at the end ("still" in bar 11) everyone (including you!) must be a musical statue until the music starts again (bar 12). The pause can be as long or as short as you like.

Teaching Tips

You can use this song with:

* movement

Hear the music and stamp your feet ...x3
or
Hear the music and jump like a frog ...x3

* actions

Hear the music and twitch your nose..x3

* percussion

Hear the music and play the bells x3

Learning Labels

* singing in unison

* memorising a melody

* listening to silence

Hear the music
Each verse ends with a game of musical statues.

Blink your eyes

An action-packed song, in which one line is changed in every verse.

Cheekily

Blink your eyes, Blow a

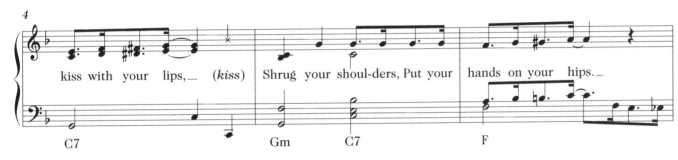

kiss with your lips,— (*kiss*) Shrug your shoul-ders, Put your hands on your hips.—

Wig - gle your bot - tom and Wig - gle your toes,_ *Put your* *fin - ger on your ear,*

And then your nose.

1. Blink your eyes,
     Blow a kiss with your lips,
   Shrug your shoulders,
     Put your hands on your hips.
   Wiggle your bottom and
     Wiggle your toes,
   Put your finger on your ear,
     And then your nose.

2. Blink your eyes,
     Blow a kiss *etc.*
   Put your finger on your tummy,
     And then your nose.

3. Blink your eyes,
     Blow a kiss *etc.*
   Put your finger on your heel,
     And then your nose.

You will need

Some active children.

How it Happens

Very straightforward — just do what the words say, while you're singing them. Choose (or ask the children to choose) a different part of the body (bar 9) each time you sing the song.

Teaching Tips

Point out to the children that the order of actions descends the body, which makes it easier to memorise.

Learning Labels

* singing in unison
* memorising a melody
* matching actions with words

Follow the leader

*This is a game of **do what I do**, set to music.*

1. **All:**

   Follow the leader,
   Do exactly what he does,
   Follow the leader now.

   Leader:

   Are you watching?

   All:

   Follow the leader,
   First he's going to press his nose,
   Then go exactly where he goes.

2. **All:**

   Follow the leader,
   Do exactly what she does,
   Follow the leader now.

   Leader:

   Are you watching?

   All:

   Follow the leader,
   First she's going to twitch her nose,
   Then go exactly where she goes.

You will need

A little space.

How it Happens

Choose a leader, who stands where everyone can see him. He chooses a suitable action to go with his nose (press, squash, flick, etc.).

Everyone sings the song, and the leader speaks his solo in rhythm (bars 11–12).

During bars 21–24, everyone presses their nose (or performs whatever the leader has chosen). Then the leader

go ex-act-ly where he goes. *Press noses:* heavier

D   A7   D   C7   F

Different action:

> > etc.   G7   C7   F   F7

A new action:

Bb   Bdim (or Bb)   F   D   G7

One more action:

Bbm   F   (Fm)   G7 C7   F   C7   F

chooses one different action for the next four bars (stamp feet, click tongue, wink an eye, blow a raspberry, etc.). The class won't know in advance what the action is going to be, and must just join in as soon as they can. The leader changes the action for the next four bars, and again for the last four.

Leading is harder than it looks!

Teaching Tips

Count out loud 1 - 8 as you perform each action, so everyone gets the feel of two beats per bar.

Interesting Ideas

* Change 'nose' in bar 16 to 'toes' and choose some suitable actions (tap, touch, squeeze, point, etc.).

* Divide the class into pairs, with one of each pair as the leader. Each partner must copy their own leader. Sing the song again, with each couple swapping over so everyone gets a turn to be leader.

Before Beginning

Play this game many times with you as the leader before asking children to lead. Use recorded music; anything with a steady beat will do.

Learning Labels

* singing in unison
* memorising a melody
* feeling and working with a steady beat

Bill's left leg

A bendy, stretchy action song, popular with little ones.

1. *Bill's left leg* moves up and down,
   From side to side and round and
   round.
   He can touch it with his fingers,
   everyone knows,
   But show us *Bill* – can you touch it
   with your nose?
   Bill's left leg moves up and down,
   From side to side and round – and
   round.

2. *Mansi's ear* moves up and down,
   From side to side and round and
   round.
   She can touch it with her fingers,
   everyone knows,
   But show us *Mansi* – can you touch it
   with your nose?
   Mansi's ear moves up and down,
   From side to side and round – and
   round.

3. *Imogen's tongue* moves up and down,
   From side to side and round and
   round.
   She can touch it with her fingers,
   everyone knows,
   But show us *Imogen* – can you touch
   it with your nose?
   Imogen's tongue moves up and down,
   From side to side and round – and
   round.

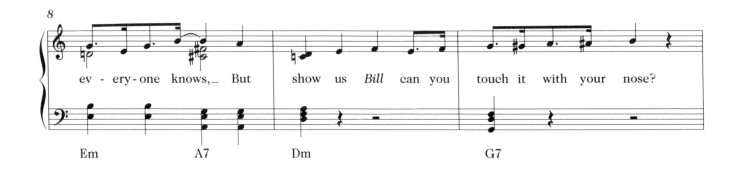

freely

play these notes in any combination until ready

a little faster

G♯dim
(or G7)

G7

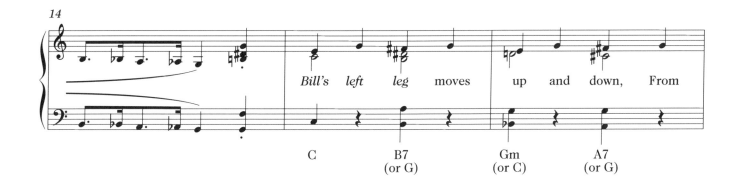

Bill's left leg moves up and down, From

C   B7   Gm   A7
         (or G)   (or C)   (or G)

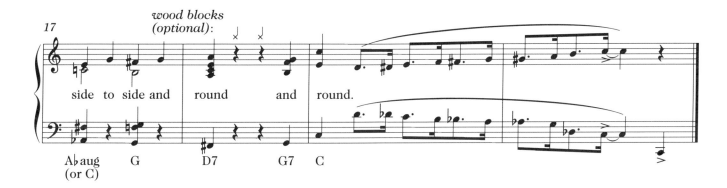

wood blocks (optional):

side to side and round and round.

A♭aug   G   D7   G7   C
(or C)

You will need

Wood blocks (if you want).

How it Happens

Change the words in the first bar each time you repeat the song. Ask a child to choose a part of their body, and use their name in the verse.

Teaching Tips

Beware of the rests in bar 18!

Try giving wood blocks (or any instrument of their choice) to a reliable child or two, with the task of playing as directed in order to remind everyone else not to sing!

Performance Points

Allow plenty of time at the chord in bar 12 for children to discover the answer (can you touch it with your nose?), but use bars 13 – 14 to bring everyone together again for the final burst.

Learning Labels

* singing in unison
* memorising a melody
* matching body movements with words

Walking
A chance to choose an alternative to walking.

1. We go walking here,
   We go walking there,
   I am feeling very tired from walking
   everywhere
   So when we're going home today
   What would you say
   If we take a helicopter all the way?

2. We go walking here,
   We go walking there,
   I am feeling very tired from walking
   everywhere
   So when we're going home today
   What would you say
   If we ride on a dragon all the way?

3. We go walking here,
   We go walking there,
   I am feeling very tired from walking
   everywhere
   So when we're going home today
   What would you say
   If we crawl on our tummies all the way?

You will need

Some space.

How it Happens

Sit still to sing the verse, then use any available space to be the helicopter, or ride on the dragon, or crawl, during the last eight bars. Ask the children to choose other ways of getting around.

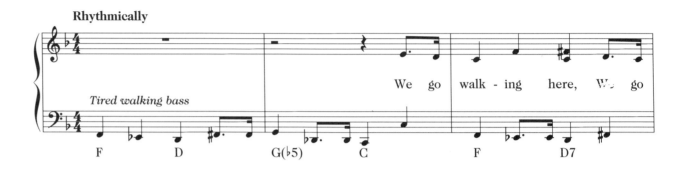

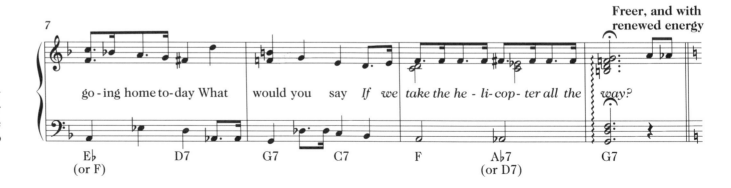

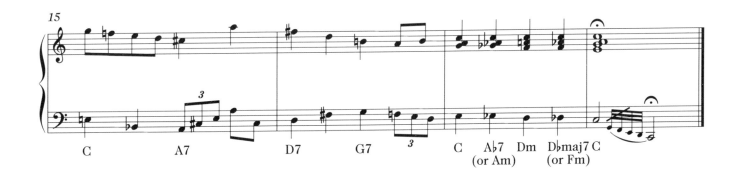

Change the rhythm in bar 9 as necessary, e.g.

drive a bus all the way

Before Beginning

Discuss means of transport:

* machines to sit in/on
* animals to ride on
* using our bodies in unusual ways etc.

Teaching Tips

Vary the accompaniment according to different methods of moving around; play faster for running, higher up the keyboard for flying, legato for rowing, etc. Try playing your version first, and ask the class to identify which means of getting around you have in mind. They may not guess the finer details, but you could give them a choice of two alternatives, and they should be able to distinguish between, say, walking on tiptoe and riding a motor bike.

Learning Labels

* singing in unison
* memorising a melody
* using the body in a variety of ways
* responding to musical mood and elements

1. Cymbals, cymbals,
Isn't it grand to play in the band on the cymbals.
Cymbals, cymbals,
Isn't it grand to play in the band on the cymbals.

2. Triangles, triangles,
Isn't it grand to play in the band on the triangles.
Triangles, triangles,
Isn't it grand to play in the band on the triangles.

3. Indian bells, Indian bells,
Isn't it grand to play in the band on the Indian bells.
Indian bells, Indian bells, etc.

Last time

Instruments, instruments,
Isn't it grand to play in the band on the instruments.
Instruments, instruments etc.

You will need

Three or four types of percussion; enough instruments for everyone to play if possible.

Use whatever instruments are available,

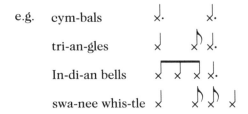

e.g. cym-bals

tri-an-gles

In-di-an bells

swa-nee whis-tle

How it Happens

Each group plays its verse in turn.

In the last verse, everyone sings and plays

Instruments

Isn't it grand

A cheery and effective song in which the percussion instruments echo the rhythm of the words.

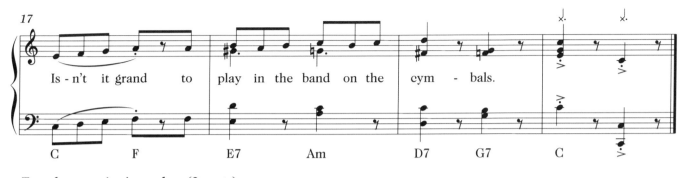

Tuned percussion/recorders (3 parts)

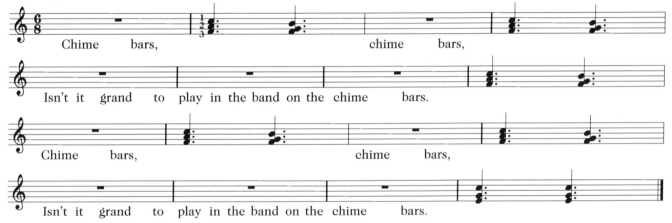

Before Beginning

Play some imitating games, where you say and clap a rhythm, and the children copy you. e.g.

you	*class*
four - teen	four - teen

you	*class*
se-ven-ty two	se-ven-ty two

Use a variety of topics: food, football teams, flowers, etc.

Also vary

* tone of voice: whisper, sing high, sing low, etc.
* actions: clap hands, tap knees, knock on the floor, etc.

Quick Questions

Clap a rhythm and ask the class which instrument it will match.

(It may match several:

goes with tri-ang-le, tam-bou-rine, cas-ta-nets, etc.)

Educational Extras

This is very effective played on tuned percussion and/or recorders. Use any or all of the three parts. Sing

glock-en-spiels

or

re - cord - ers

or whatever is appropriate, and change the rhythm accordingly.

Teaching Tips

Introduce the song using body percussion instead of instruments.

Sing:

Clap your hands

tap your toes

Isn't it grand to play in the band when you

bang your fists   etc.

For Fun

Choose six children and give each one a different instrument, but don't tell the rest of the class who has what. Use a screen or other secrecy aid. Each of the six children has responsibility for one of the following bars: 1, 3, 7, 9, 11, 15.

These *were* the bars which named the instruments, but now they become instrumental bars.

The rest of the class has to respond in bars 2, 4, 8, 10, 12, and 16 by singing the name of the instrument they heard in the previous bar.

Build up to this game gently, using one or two instruments at first.

Learning Labels

* singing in unison
* memorising a melody
* imitation of rhythm, pitch, tone of voice
* using a variety of tuned and untuned percussion, and recorders
* playing and identifying specific rhythmic patterns
* identifying instruments according to their timbre

We can pretend

Each percussion instrument represents an everyday (or not so everyday) sound.

1. *Click* go the *castanets*,
   Click go the *castanets*,
   Listen to their sound.
   We can pretend the sound they make
      are
   Crocodiles all around.

2. *Whoosh* go the *whistles*,
   Whoosh go the *whistles*,
   Listen to their sound.
   We can pretend the sound they make
      is the
   Wind all around.

3. *Clash* go the *cymbals*,
   Clash go the *cymbals*,
   Listen to their sound.
   We can pretend the sound they make
      are
   Tractors all around.

Last time

   Play on your instruments,
   Play on your instruments,
   Listen to their sound.
   We can pretend the sound they make
      are
   Different things all around.

You will need

Any variety of percussion instruments; whatever is appropriate and available.

How it Happens

Sing the song, changing the words in bars 3, 4 and 9 as necessary. Then play the percussion during the last eight bars of accompaniment.

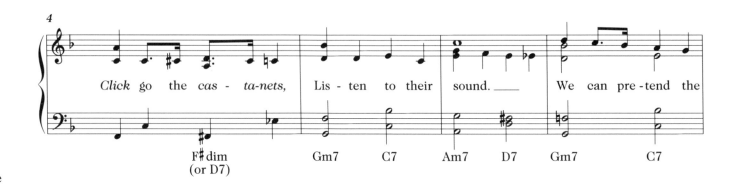

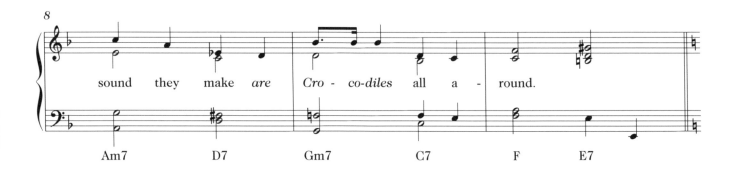

Percussion starts:

11   *etc.*

Am   A7   Dm   G(aug)   C

15

Dm   Fm   Em   A7   Dm   G7   C

Teaching Tips

Sometimes the sound will be rhythmic (horses' hooves); sometimes it won't (car horns in a traffic jam). Encourage the children to play their instruments realistically according to what they are pretending to be.

Before Beginning

Stretch the imagination by discussing how musical sounds can represent the sounds of other things.

Educational Extras

Find ways to make the eight instrumental bars more interesting. Try these:

* wood blocks represent a ticking clock which stops mid-verse

* a guiro represents a croaking frog which dives into the pond, and then re-emerges (two bars rest)

* Indian bells represent the milkman who approaches, then passes by (⊲ ⊳)

* a drum represents feet which run, walk, scamper, stamp, jump, etc.

Learning Labels

* singing in unison
* memorising a melody
* improvising, both rhythmically and freely
* selecting and using a range of percussion
* awareness of pace, timbre, dynamics, silence

1. *This is the sound of the drum,*
   Playing loud and clear.
   It makes its sound with a steady beat –
   It makes you want to start tapping
        your feet.
   This is the sound of the drum
   Playing for everyone to hear.

2. *This is the sound of the tambourine,*
   Playing loud and clear.
   It makes its sound with a steady beat –
   It makes you want to start tapping
        your feet.
   This is the sound of the tambourine
   Playing for everyone to hear.

Last time

   This is the sound of the band,
   Playing loud and clear.
   It makes its sound with a steady beat –
   It makes you want to start tapping
        your feet.
   This is the sound of the band
   Playing for everyone to hear.

You will need

Three or four types of percussion, e.g. drums, tambourines, cymbals, wood blocks, (or whatever is available). Give everyone an instrument.

How it Happens

After singing the verse, the percussion is played to an agreed rhythm, as an *ostinato* (a repetitive rhythmic pattern).

Teaching Tips

Decide before singing each verse which rhythm your instrumentalists will play.

The sound of the band

A lilting, lyrical melody in waltz tempo which encourages the use of rhythms in $\frac{3}{4}$.

Percussion begins:

24 ... Play-ing for ev-'ry-one to hear.

D7 · Gm7 · C7 · F · C7 · F · C

31 ... F · D7 · Gm · C7 · F

38 ... F(aug) · Bb · Gm(b5) (or Bbm) · F · C7 · F

Here are some possibilities:

drums   This is the sound

tambourines   Stea - dy beat

cymbals   clear   clear

wood blocks   wood blocks play-ing for

Before Beginning

Play some games in which the children clap the rhythm of words,

e.g.   I'm wear-ing   blue

or

I'm   in yel-low   etc.

If they're good at it, split into two (or more) parts and say the words and clap the rhythms at the same time. Use other body percussion too (tap knees, nod head, etc.) and use a conductor to indicate changes in volume or speed.

Performance Points

Each group of players performs its own verse, then as a finale *This is the sound of the band* includes everyone. In the instrumental break, if your band can manage it, each group plays the ostinato they rehearsed. If that's too tricky, decide on a rhythm to be played in unison by all instruments

e.g.   sound of the band

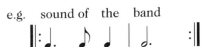

Learning Labels

* singing in unison
* memorising a melody
* choosing and using an ostinato accompaniment
* using a variety of untuned percussion instruments

One musician in the band

A pyramid-selling song: the band starts with one musician, then grows to two, then four, then eight, etc.

1. We've got *one* musician in the band today,
   One musician in the band.
   Watch and listen as she plays her instrument –
   One musician in the band.
   > Let's find a way to make the sound louder.
   > Choose a musician to come and lend a hand.

2. We've got *two* musicians in the band today,
   Two musicians in the band
   Watch and listen as they play their instruments –
   Two musicians in the band.
   > Let's find a way to make the sound louder.
   > Choose a musician to come and lend a hand.

3. We've got *four* musicians in the band today,
   Four musicians in the band.
   Watch and listen as they play their instruments –
   Four musicians in the band.
   > Let's find a way to make the sound louder.
   > Choose a musician to come and lend a hand.

Last time
   > We've got *all our* musicians in the band today,
   > *All our* musicians in the band.
   > Watch and listen as we play our instruments –
   > *All our* musicians in the band.

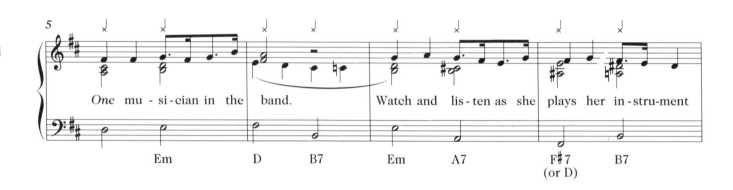

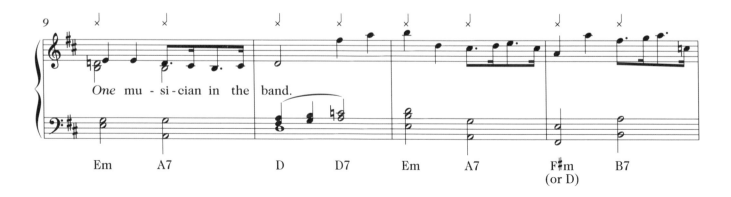

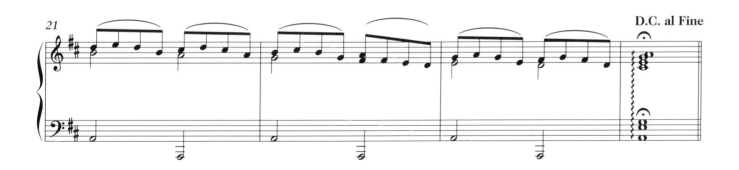

You will need

Some space

Enough untuned percussion for everyone to play.

How it Happens

Invite one musician to start the band, and ask her to choose an instrument.

Everyone sings, while she plays as directed in the song.

During the *choosing music* she invites a friend to join her, the friend chooses an instrument, and you begin again, this time with *Two musicians in the band today*. Therefore in each subsequent verse the number of musicians is doubled.

Teaching Tips

If the class is large, start with two or even three musicians – that way everyone gets a turn sooner.

If you like, you can adapt the length of the *choosing music* to suit the childrens' needs: just cut it short or extend it as appropriate and bring it to a close with a chord of A7.

The basic rhythm could be varied *ad lib.* by the performers, if you like.

For Fun

The children can walk around in any available space while they're playing their instruments, stopping each time at bar 14.

Learning Labels

* singing in unison
* memorising a melody
* awareness of volume increase
* selecting from a range of percussion instruments

Improvising on my instrument

Here is an opportunity to improvise using any sound source.

Improvising on my instrument,
Doesn't matter what I use.
Improvising on my instrument,
Listen to the sounds I choose.

You will need

Any sound source that you or the children choose. Use tuned or untuned percussion, recorders, classroom objects, junk materials — anything at all that makes a noise.

How it Happens

Everyone has a turn, either as soloist or in a small group, first to sing the verse and then to improvise during the last 16 bars.

Before Beginning

Explain the joys of improvising; you can play exactly what you want! Encourage interesting playing: contrasts between fast and slow, loud and quiet; stopping in the middle for a short rest, etc.

There's only one rule: you have to stop at the end, so keep listening all the way through.

Teaching Tips

When playing tuned instruments use the notes in the pentatonic scale of G (DE GAB).

Remove all the Cs and Fs from the instruments so that children have the freedom to play all the remaining notes.

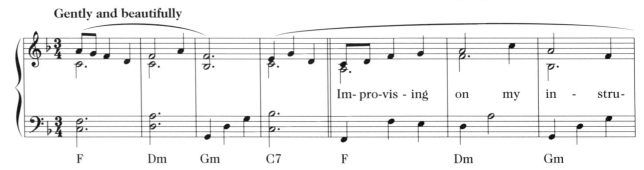

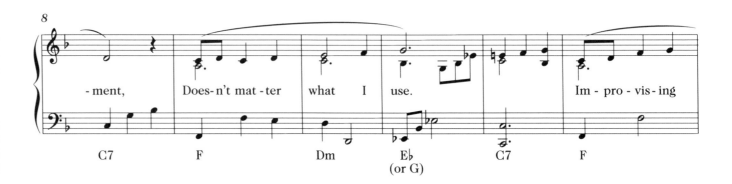

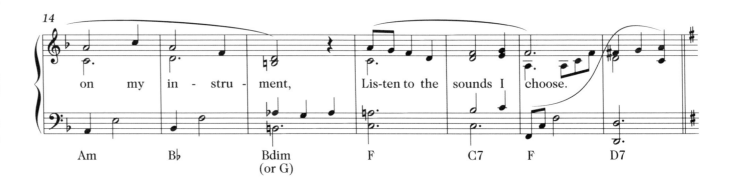

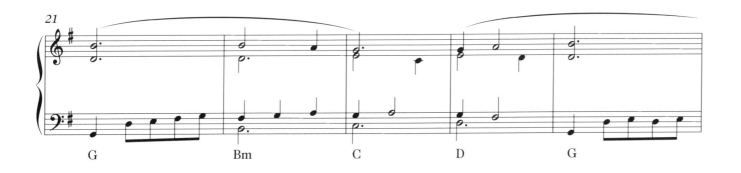

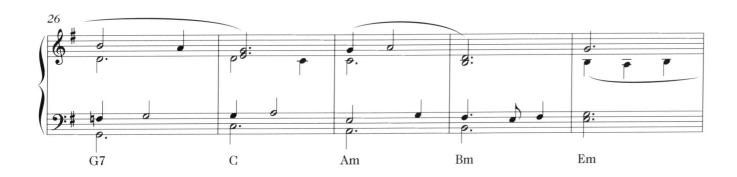

Interesting Ideas

Consider using categories of sound sources,

e.g. plastic objects (rulers, yoghurt pots, etc.)

paper (tissue, cardboard)

wood

metal

childrens' own bodies, etc.

Encourage the children to discover as many different ways as possible of making sounds:

tapping, scraping, tearing, rubbing, blowing on or into, wobbling, etc.

Learning Labels

* singing in small groups or solo
* memorising a melody
* experiencing freedom of expression, both in choosing a sound source and deciding how to play it

Me and you, what shall we do? *A rhyme with actions.*

1, 2,
me and you,
what shall we do?

3, 4,
touch the floor,
do it once more.

5, 6,
cement to mix,
lay those bricks.

7, 8,
open the gate,
wave to your mate.

9, 10,
do it again?
yes!

(Whispered at first, then getting louder)
1, 2,
me and you,
what shall we do?

3, 4, etc.....

9, 10,
do it again?
NO!

You will need
A little space.

How it Happens
Say the rhyme and perform the actions.

Teaching Tips
Don't let the rhyme slow down; keep the beat going. It may help to play a drum on the strong beats (each new line).

Performance Points
Choose soloists or small groups to chant the numbers, and/or the replies.

Educational Extras
Try it like this:
* First time spoken, second time $pp < ff$
or
* whispered
* silent (actions only)
* starting slowly (*lento*), then gradually getting faster (*presto*)

For Fun
Recite the numbers backwards and ask the children to find rhyming phrases,
e.g. 10, 9
Sun-shine,
Weather is fine. etc.

Learning Labels
* rhythmic speaking in unison/solo/small groups
* feeling and keeping to a steady pulse
* awareness of dynamics, pace, silence

Knees Clap *A versatile rhythmic chant.*

Knees clap – finger,
Knees clap – 2,
Knees clap – cow horns,
Knees clap – moo!

Knees clap – nostril,
Knees clap – 2,
Knees clap – smelly?
Knees clap – pooh!

Knees clap – 1 size,
Knees clap – 2,
Knees clap – shrinking,
Knees clap – grew!

Knees clap – 1 wing,
Knees clap – 2,
Knees clap – albatross,
Knees clap – cuckoo!

Knees clap – 1 hand,
Knees clap – 2,
Knees clap – caught the ball,
Knees clap – threw!

Knees clap – colour,
Knees clap – 2,
Knees clap – red,
Knees clap – blue!

Knees clap – 1 sleeve,
Knees clap – 2,
Knees clap – T shirt,
Knees clap – shoe!

Knees clap – 1 paw,
Knees clap – 2,
Knees clap – kanga,
Knees clap – roo.

Knees clap – person,
Knees clap – 2,
Knees clap – me,
Knees clap – you!

Knees clap – 1 nod,
Knees clap – 2,
Knees clap – don't,
Knees clap – do!

Knees clap – 1 tooth,
Knees clap – 2,
Knees clap – swallow,
Knees clap – chew!

Knees clap – 1 snake,
Knees clap – 2,
Knees clap – giraffe,
Knees clap – ZOO!

You will need

Some children

How it Happens

Each verse lasts for the equivalent of four bars in 4/4.

Knees clap comes on the first two beats of each bar, and you tap knees then clap hands correspondingly. The other words fit in during the rest of the bar.

Incorporate the actions throughout; they are part of the rhyme.

The order of verses in unimportant, except for the final ZOO. At the end of that verse, everyone shouts 'zoo', and all make a brief animal sound (any variety) as a finale.

Before Beginning

Play this rhythm game with the childrens' own names. Sit in a circle and get the basic rhythm going

When that is steady, each child in turn says their name during the rests,

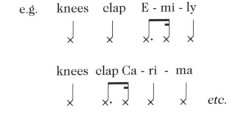

Begin with everyone saying all the names. As confidence increases, many children will be able to speak on their own.

Change from names to:

* musical instruments
* places
* parts of the body etc.

Teaching Tips

Keep the beat going with a very steady pulse throughout and make sure "knees clap" comes in exactly the right place every time. That will make it easier to put in the other words.

When learning and performing the rhyme, keep things going by saying (and doing) this rhythm,

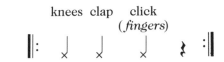

as often as necessary between each verse.

Performance Points

Perform the actions for "knees clap" but leave out those words.

Alternatively, everyone says/performs "knees clap" but choose a soloist or small group to say and perform the rest of each verse.

For Fun

Invite the class to make up their own verses, or variations on these.

Learning Labels

* rhythmic speaking in unison/solo/small groups
* feeling and keeping to a steady pulse
* inserting words and actions into a defined space

Group 1 ABCD,

Do you want to spell with me?

Group 2 DEFG,

I would rather eat my tea.

1 You must learn to read and write.

2 I'll just have another bite.

1 & 2 ABCDEFG

1 } Spell with me.

2 } Eat my tea.

You will need

At least two tuned percussion instruments, one for each part. It is even better if you have more instruments.

How it Happens

Split the class into two groups, 1 and 2. Sing the song as directed. Depending on how many instruments are available, members from each group play the notes in bars 3, 5, and 10.

Teaching Tips

To make life easier for the players, remove the two notes on either side of those to be played:

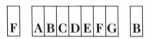

Before playing, give the children some practice at feeling where the instrumental bars are, and at how the speed varies

(first ♩ ♩ ♩ ♩ then ♫ ♫ ♫ ♩).

Sing the song, and put in claps, or taps, etc. (in the correct rhythms) in bars 3, 5, and 10.

A B C D

A song in two parts which incorporates tuned percussion in a simple and effective way. The speed of the song is dictated by how fast the children can play bar 10 on tuned percussion.

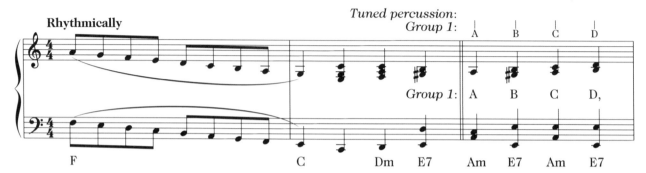

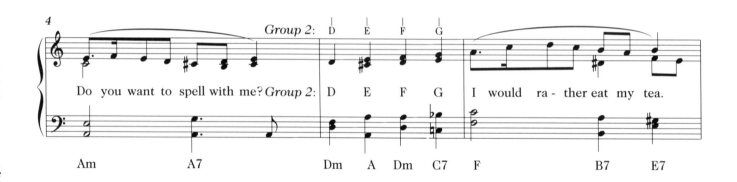

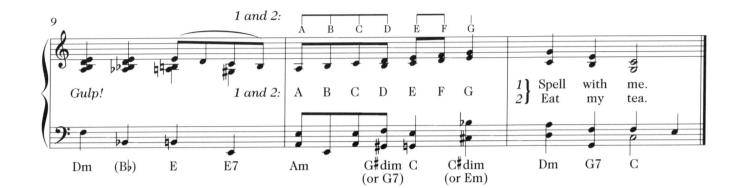

Help the class by keeping to the same tempo throughout. Don't wait for either group to sing their lines. Encourage them to come in on time with each phrase.

Performance Points

Sing first, then sing and play, finally play without words.

Educational Extras

Add ♪ to both percussion parts in the last bar.

For Fun

Encourage group 2 to make a noisy swallow on the 'gulp' in bar 9, but be strict and ensure it only lasts for one beat.

Learning Labels

* singing in two parts
* memorising a melody
* playing a simple melody on tuned percussion
* becoming familiar with note names and the layout of notes on tuned percussion instruments

Going to the playground

Here children have the opportunity to play descriptive sounds on tuned percussion.

1. Going to the playground,
   Up the steps we run,
   Stand on the top step of the slide,
   Sliding down is fun.

2. Going to the playground,
   To the swings we run,
   Sit on the seat, go there and back,
   Swinging high is fun.

3. Going to the playground,
   To the see-saw we run,
   You're going up as I go down,
   See-sawing is fun.

You will need

At least three tuned percussion instruments. Use more if you have them. (One instrument could be shared between three children — one playing each verse.)

How it Happens

After singing each verse, a soloist or small group plays the appropriate music. The verse can be sung by everyone, or by the players alone.

Teaching Tips

Encourage the children to play the notes with a finger before using beaters, and they can sing as they touch the note (an approximation of high/low/moving upwards, etc. is enough to give a feeling of changing pitch — don't expect every note to be sung in tune or played exactly as suggested here).

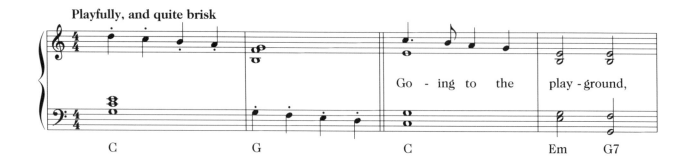

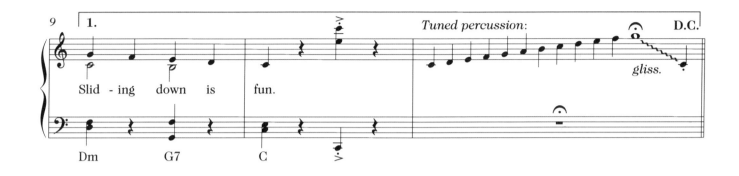

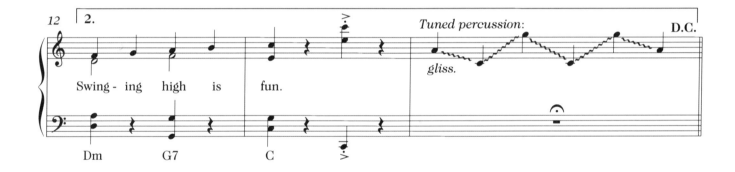

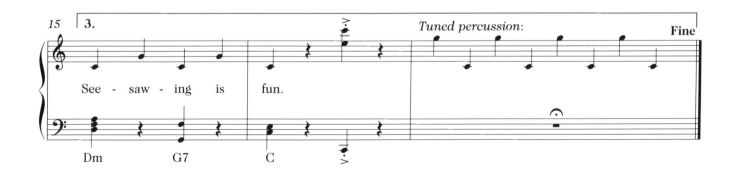

Quick Questions

Can the children identify each instrumental snippet when it's played:

* without the verse
* while their eyes are shut

For Fun

Use any other percussion instruments as well (or instead if you prefer),

e.g. a tambourine tapped as the steps of the slide are climbed, then shaken to represent sliding down.

Learning Labels

* singing in unison/small groups
* memorising a melody
* using tuned percussion to play descriptive music
* matching the concept of high/low with corresponding pitches

I am!

A versatile question and answer song which can be used with actions or percussion.

1. **Question**
   Who is tapping shoulders today?
   Answer
   I am! I am!
   Question
   Who is getting ready to play?
   Answer
   I am so listen to me.

2. **Question**
   Who is holding castanets today?
   Answer
   I am! I am!
   Question
   Who is getting ready to play?
   Answer
   I am so listen to me.

3. **Question**
   Who is holding an instrument today?
   Answer
   I am! I am!
   Question
   Who is getting ready to play?
   Answer
   I am so listen to me.

You will need

Any mixture of percussion instruments.

How it Happens

Sing the song (both questions and answers), then whoever has answered performs their chosen activity during the last eight bars of accompaniment.

They may either play to a steady beat:

or improvise their own rhythms (see opposite).

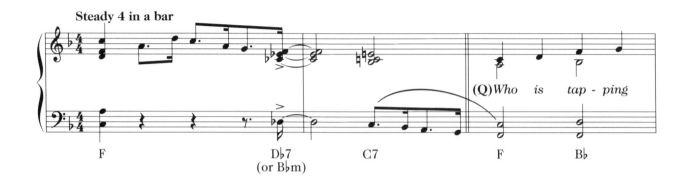

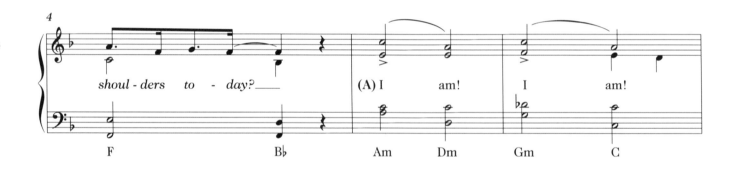

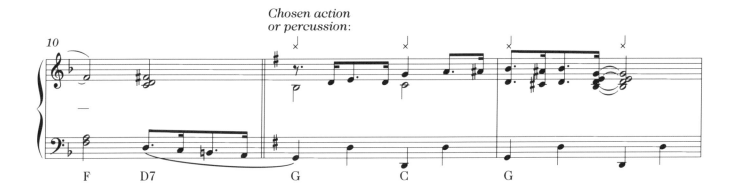

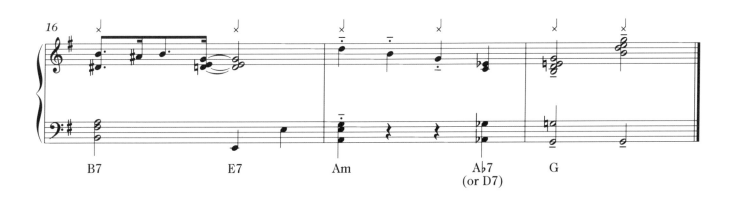

The song can be split in many different ways:

question	answer
you	the class
half the class	the other half
most of the class	a soloist or small group, etc.

Teaching Tips

First teach the responses (bars 5 & 6, 9 & 10) by asking the class to copy you in a variety of ways: say the words, whisper them, mouth them, shout them, etc.

After you've sung a few verses with you asking the questions and the class singing the answers, they'll know the questions well enough to sing them for you to reply.

Change the words as you wish:

> Who is clicking their tongue today?
> Who is holding a triangle today? etc.

Educational Extras

Instead of using the rhythm "I am, I am", in bars 11–18, make up some alternatives.

Try these:

Learning Labels

* singing in unison
* singing and playing solo and in small groups
* memorising a melody
* imitating rhythmic patterns
* choosing, using and developing simple rhythms

1. **Both groups (leaders and followers):**
   1 2 3 *clap!*
   1 2 3 *clap!*
   First count the numbers and
   then *clap your hands* like this,
   1 2 3 *clap!*
   1 2 3 *clap!*
   First count the numbers and
   then *clap your hands.*

   leaders: 1 2 3
   followers: 1 2 3
   leaders: 1 2 3
   followers: 1 2 3 etc.
   (last two bars:)
   leaders: 1
   followers: 1

2. 1 2 3 *tap!*
   1 2 3 *tap!*
   First count the numbers and
   then *tap the drum* like this, *etc.*

You will need

Any mixture of percussion instruments.

How it Happens

Split the class into two groups: leaders and followers. The groups can be equal in size or not, as you wish. Everyone sings and claps in the first 16 bars.

For the rest of the song the two groups clap alternate bars.

Teaching Tips

First sing the second half without any actions but alternating leaders and followers, then try clapping alternate bars. When the children are good at this, add other actions, and then percussion instruments.

Begin with you as leader, and the class following. As confidence and familiarity grow, choose leaders from the class. Encourage the leaders to start clapping as their bars begin, and not to be late

1 2 3 clap
A gentle waltz in which leaders and followers share 3/4 rhythms. (This is surprisingly hard and may be too difficult for younger children.)

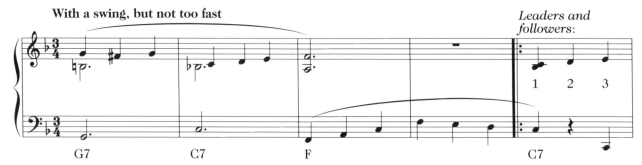

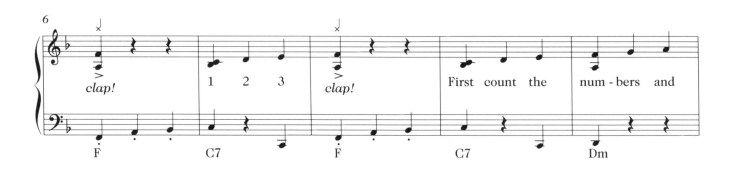

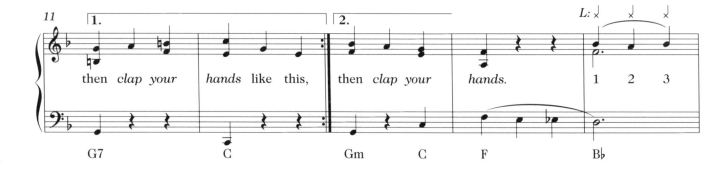

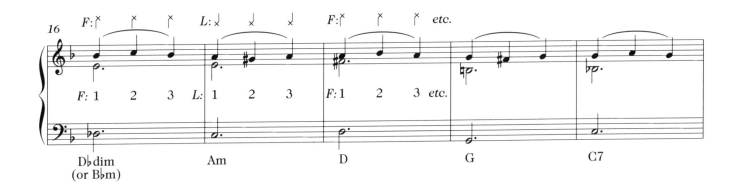

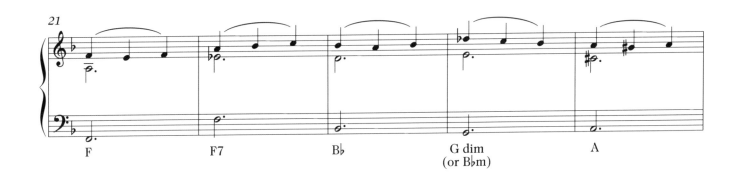

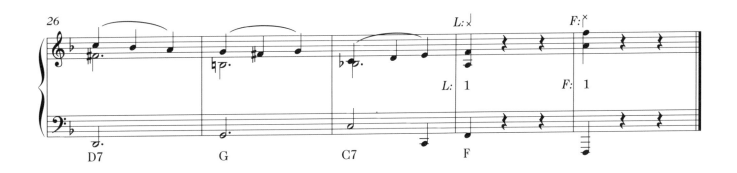

entering. The game is easier if the leader keeps to one rhythm throughout.

Performance Points

Don't just clap. Use any action — or instrument. Change the words as necessary:

* 1 2 3 shake or 1 2 3 scrape etc.

Before Beginning

Play some copying games in $\frac{3}{4}$. Vary your actions in each bar: clap hands, tap knees, knock on your head, etc.

Educational Extras

Vary the last 16 bars so that the followers have to listen carefully:

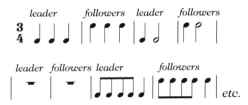

When you do this, use a solo leader, not a group.

Then add dynamics.

Learning Labels

* singing in unison
* memorising a melody
* imitating rhythmic patterns
* using a range of percussion instruments
* awareness of duration, dynamics, silence

Have you heard the news?

An opportunity to play on the off-beats.

2 4 6 8 10 and 12
Have you heard the news?
We can count in twos.
2 4 6 8 10 and 12
We can count in twos like this.

1 2 **3** 4 **5** 6 **7** 8 **9** **10** 11 **12**
Headline news!
1 2 **3** 4 **5** 6 **7** 8 **9** **10** 11 **12**
We can count in twos!

2 4 6 8 10 and 12
Have you heard the news?
We can count in twos.
2 4 6 8 10 and 12
We can count in twos like this.

You will need

Any mixture of percussion instruments.

How it Happens

Everyone sings the chorus.

During bars 11–13, count aloud from 1 to 12.

Everyone claps on numbers 2, 4, 6, 8, 10 and 12 (the off-beats), then shouts "Head-line news", as if selling newspapers.

During bars 15–17, count the numbers and clap on the off-beats, then shout 'We can count in twos'.

Then it's back to bar 3 to repeat the first section.

You can take the song round (first section, second section, and back to the first) as many times as you like, using a different action or instrument each time you repeat the second section.

— 34 —

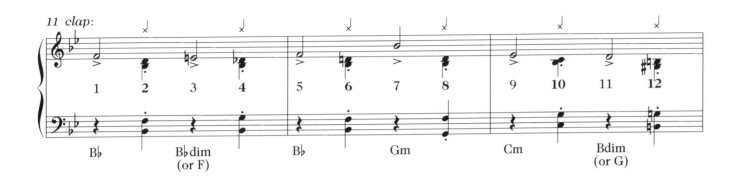

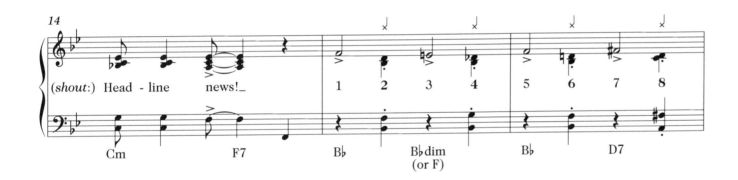

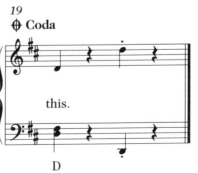

D.S. 𝄋 then Coda

Teaching Tips

If children find it difficult to clap on the weak beats, encourage them to bring their hands apart in a clearly defined movement on the strong beats in between.

Before Beginning

Give the children plenty of practice using off-beats. Play any recorded music that has a strong beat and lead the children doing actions on the weak beats. Quite difficult!

(Reggae music has a strong off-beat, and could be suitable.)

For Fun

At the end of the song, whisper

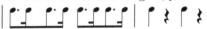

and then repeat the whole song.

Learning Labels

* singing in unison
* memorising a melody
* feeling and using off-beats
* using a range of percussion instruments

Different ways

An excellent song for exploring contrast in music.

Slow and lyrical

1. Loudly, quietly,
   Loudly, quietly,
   Playing in different ways.
   Loudly, quietly,
   Loudly, quietly,
   Playing in different ways.

e.g.

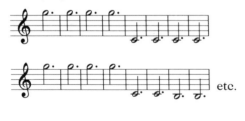

etc.

2. Fast, then slowly,
   Fast, then slowly,
   Playing in different ways.
   Fast, then slowly,
   Fast, then slowly,
   Playing in different ways.

e.g.

etc.

3. High notes, low notes,
   High notes, low notes,
   Playing in different ways,
   High notes, low notes,
   High notes, low notes,
   Playing in different ways.

etc.

Fm   B♭7   E♭   D7   G   C

B7   Gm   Am   D7   G

You will need

Any mixture of instruments.

How it Happens

Sing and play as directed in the song. During the second half, from bar 21 to the end, the contrasts are demonstrated. Each contrasting section lasts for four bars, but the rhythms used within the four bars can vary as you wish.

The most basic rhythm is

You could use the words of each verse to help find an alternative rhythm, e.g.

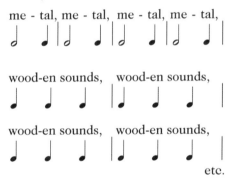

me - tal, me - tal, me - tal, me - tal,

wood-en sounds,   wood-en sounds,

wood-en sounds,   wood-en sounds,

etc.

Choose actions or instruments, whichever is appropriate to the words you choose.

Learning Labels

* singing in unison
* memorising a melody
* choosing and using rhythms
* using a range of instruments
* awareness of pitch, duration, pace, timbre, texture, dynamics, silence

Teaching Tips

Either organise everyone to play from bar 21 to the end, or split the class into two groups, one to demonstrate each contrast. In that way, each group plays alternate four bar phrases.

Help the performers by matching the accompaniment to their chosen words.

Change the rhythm too, if necessary,

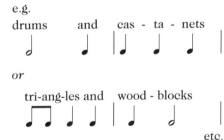

e.g.

drums   and   cas - ta - nets

or

tri-ang-les and   wood - blocks

etc.

Before Beginning

How many contrasting pairs can your class find? Here are some ideas:

many sounds — one sound
strong — gentle
noisy — silent
quietly — quieter
metal sounds — wooden sounds
piercing — soothing
fast and loud — slow and loud

While you sing this song

A simple and adaptable song to use with movement, actions, or percussion.

1. *Clap your hands* while you sing this song,
   Clap your hands while you sing this song,
   Clap your hands while you sing this song,
   And now choose something else to do
   While you're singing along.

2. *Shrug one shoulder* while you sing this song,
   Shrug one shoulder while you sing this song,
   Shrug one shoulder while you sing this song,
   And now choose something else to do
   While you're singing along.

3. *Exercise your elbows* while you sing this song,
   Exercise your elbows while you sing this song,
   Exercise your elbows while you sing this song,

Last time
   And now there's nothing else to do
   While you're singing along.

You will need

Some space (if you want).

Any mixture of percussion instruments.

How it Happens

Choose any activity to do while you sing the song, a different one for each verse. If you suggest the first few, the children will probably come up with the rest.

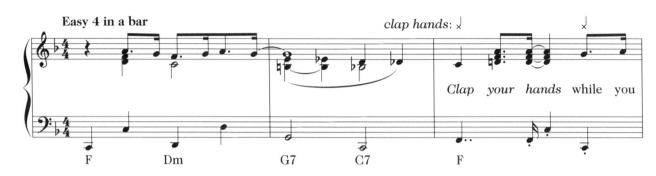

Teaching Tips

You can use this song with:

* movement
flutter like a butterfly while you sing this song, *or*
take giant steps while you sing this song
* actions
blink your eyes, *or*
wave your arms
* percussion
play the tambourine, *or*
beat the drum

Performance Points

Very small children may find it difficult to sing and perform an action simultaneously. You could split the class into two groups, one to sing and the other to perform.

Educational Extras

Try these:
* Clap very quietly. . .
* Make a crescendo. . .
* Play slow beats. . .
* Play a dotted rhythm. . .
. . . and any other variations which are suitable for the class.

Learning Labels

* singing in unison
* memorising a melody
* making decisions
* dynamic contrasts
* duration of note lengths

1. **Question**
   What is the best way to make a *clappy*
     sound,
   The best way to make a *clappy*
     sound?
   Answer
   I'll use my *hands* 'cos I have found
   That's the best way to make a *clappy*
     sound.

2. **Question**
   What is the best way to make a *tingy*
     sound,
   The best way to make a *tingy* sound?
   Answer
   I'll use the *bells* 'cos I have found
   That's the best way to make a *tingy*
     sound.

3. **Question**
   What is the best way to make a *growly*
     sound,
   The best way to make a *growly* sound?
   Answer
   I'll use my *voice* 'cos I have found
   That's the best way to make a *growly*
     sound.

Last time
   Question
   What is the best way to make a *mixed-
     up* sound,
   The best way to make a *mixed-up*
     sound?
   Answer
   We'll use *everything* 'cos we have
     found
   That's the best way to make a *mixed-
     up* sound.

You will need

Anything at all that makes a sound, e.g.
bodies, instruments, classroom objects,
saucepan lids, comb and paper, paper to
tear, etc.

The best way

A question and answer song which explores the widest range of sound sources. The possibilities are endless.

13

Em   A7   D7   G   (G#dim)

16

D   B7   Em   A7   D

How it Happens

Any sized group can sing either question or answer (you/the rest, half/half, majority/ small group or soloist). After singing the answer, that group demonstrates the sound source of their choice during the last eight bars of accompaniment. They can either play to a steady minim beat, or improvise their own rhythms.

Tuned percussion and recorders can be used, playing an A throughout (and a B in bar 15 if the players are able).

Teaching Tips

Before singing each verse decide on both the sound source and the description,

e.g.   wood blocks   —   clicky
       elastic band   —   twangy
       bowl of water   —   splashy

Learning Labels

* singing in unison
* singing in small groups or solo
* memorising a melody
* improvising both vocally and instrumentally
* finding and using an inexhaustible range of sound sources
* awareness and consideration of pitch, timbre, texture, dynamics, silence

Educational Extras

Sort the sound sources into groups:
* metal/wood/skin
* natural/synthetic
* loud/quiet/variable

For Fun

What is the best way to make a silent sound?
I'll keep very still 'cos I have found . . .

Quick Questions

Ask the children to identify sounds before they have seen the sound source. Drums may be easy enough, but try sharpening a pencil, or slamming a lid.

Then ask them to find an adjective which describes the sound.

Before Beginning

Discuss the vocabulary of adjectives which describe sound: noisy, loud, quiet, gentle, etc. but also: ugly, frightening, funny, tinkly, squeaky, low, silent, etc.

1. **Everyone:**
   Tom is standing in the middle of the
      circle,
   What's he going to do?
   Tom:
   I am going to *tap my tummy*
   And you can do it too.

2. **Everyone:**
   Nalini's standing in the middle of the
      circle,
   What's she going to do?
   Nalini:
   I am going to *whistle a tune*
   And you can do it too.

You will need

Some space

Any mixture of percussion instruments.

How it Happens

One child stands in the middle of the circle, or classroom, or musicroom, or carpet (change the words in the song as appropriate).

The others sing the question, and the soloist replies.

Everyone performs the chosen action during the last eight bars of accompaniment, either to a steady beat, or improvising a rhythm.

Teaching Tips

You can use this song with:

* movement
I am going to jump up high
* actions
I am going to knock my kneecaps

Middle of the circle

For children who love to be in the centre of things.

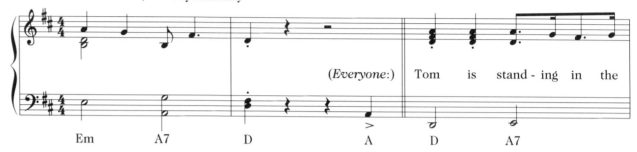

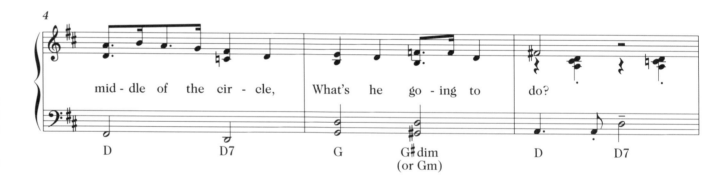

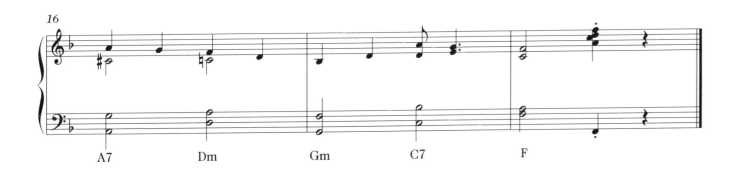

I am going to shake the maracas

You can put more than one child in the middle, and sing

"These two are standing in the middle of the circle . . ."

or "Six people standing . . ." etc.

Educational Extras

If the rhythm of the chosen action is suitable, say or sing the soloist's name to this rhythm during the last eight bars.

or

or

Ask the soloist to choose a dynamic pattern, e.g.

and ask the rest of the class to match it by watching and listening.

Learning Labels

* singing in unison
* singing a solo
* memorising a melody
* making decisions
* choosing and using simple rhythms
* awareness of dynamics

Ready steady play

Choose a subject, and all the children who identify with it can play their instrument.

1. *Have you got a hamster*
   Who's furry and squeaky and brown?
   If you've got a hamster
   It's your turn to play
   So get ready to play,
   Ready steady to play today.

2. *Have you been to the seaside*
   And had a good splash in the sea?
   If you've been to the seaside
   It's your turn to play
   So get ready to play,
   Ready steady to play today.

3. *Are you wearing trousers,*
   To keep your legs wonderfully warm?
   If you're wearing trousers
   It's your turn to play
   So get ready to play,
   Ready steady to play today.

4. *Do you like to see fireworks*
   Which light up the sky when it's dark?
   If you like to see fireworks
   It's your turn to play
   So get ready to play,
   Ready steady to play today.

You will need

Any mixture of percussion; enough instruments for everyone to play.

How it Happens

Everyone has an instrument ready to play. One person chooses a subject (you may have to help with the words in bars 9–12). Sing the song, then the appropriate people play their instruments from bar 25 to the end.

play, Read-y stead-y to play to - day.

Teaching Tips

Use diverse topics:

* Are you holding a tambourine, that's round with jingly bells?

* Do you like spaghetti, all covered and smothered in sauce?

* Can you do a cartwheel, and turn right around on your hands?

Educational Extras

Choose a structure for the 16 instrumental bars:

* a plan using dynamics: *ff*, *pp*,

or $\diamondleft\hspace{-2pt}=\hspace{-2pt}\diamondright$

* a rhythmic pattern:

read - y, stead - y

Grade your structure according to the ability of the class.

Quick Questions

Can anyone find a topic which:

* includes everyone in the room

* excludes everyone in the room

* includes only two children   etc.

Learning Labels

* singing in unison

* memorising a melody

* making decisions

* awareness of texture: different combinations of instruments

Let's try it and see
Can the children manage to do two things at once?

1. Can you clap your hands while you
   stand on one foot?
   Can you clap your hands while you
   stand on one foot?
   Can you clap your hands while you
   stand on one foot?
   Let's try it and see.

2. Can you blink your eyes while you're
   flapping your arms?
   Can you blink your eyes while you're
   flapping your arms?
   Can you blink your eyes while you're
   flapping your arms?
   Let's try it and see.

3. Can you pull your ears while you're
   rubbing your knees?
   Can you pull your ears while you're
   rubbing your knees?
   Can you pull your ears while you're
   rubbing your knees?
   Let's try it and see.

You will need

Some space (if you want).

Any mixture of percussion instruments.

How it Happens

Sing the song, then try out the combination of actions while the accompaniment is repeated. Where appropriate, perform the actions to a steady minim beat.

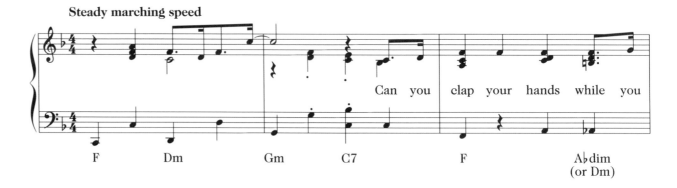

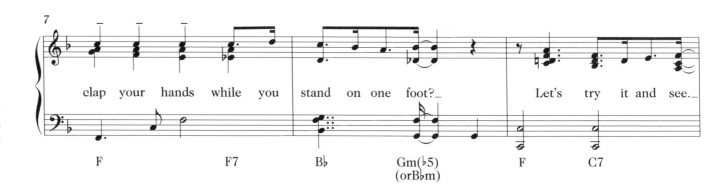

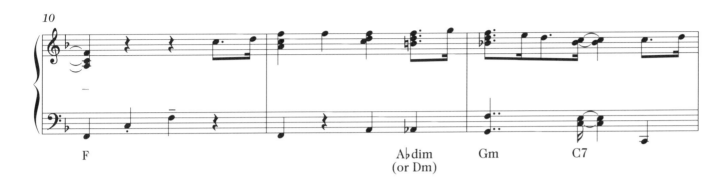

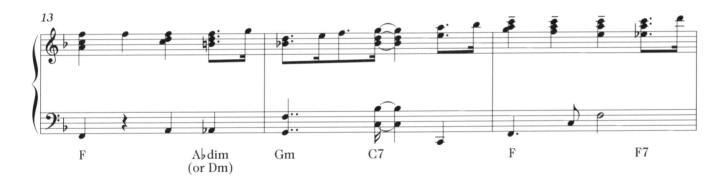

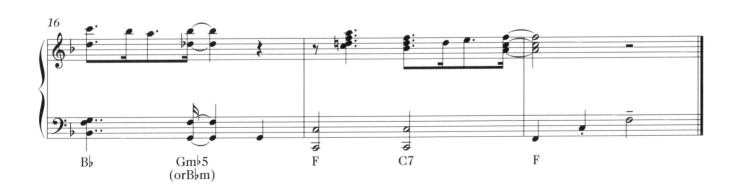

Teaching Tips

The children may try to perform the actions while they sing the verse, and both will suffer! Encourage them to sing first, *then* perform. Try a game of hiding hands away while singing.

Educational Extras

Try as many combinations as you like:

Can you	*while you*
nod your head	kneel on the floor
shrug your shoulders	tiptoe around
beat the drum	walk in a circle
play the castanets	stick out your tongue
play very quietly	blink your eyes

Learning Labels

* singing in unison
* memorising a melody
* making decisions
* using a range of percussion instruments

Sing to the music
A simple song for little ones.

1. *Clap your hands* and sing to the music,
   Clap your hands and sing to the song,
   Clap your hands and sing along,
   Sing along to the song.

2. *Take giant steps* and sing to the music,
   Take giant steps and sing to the song,
   Take giant steps and sing along,
   Sing along to the song.

3. *Play the castanets* and sing to the
       music,
   Play the castanets and sing to the song,
   Play the castanets and sing along,
   Sing along to the song.

You will need

Some space (if you want).

Any mixture of percussion instruments.

How it Happens

Choose any action (gnash your teeth, jump up high, etc.) and perform it while you sing the song.

Add instruments if you like.

Educational Extras

Try these:

* clap very quietly and sing to the music

* clap a little louder

* clap very loudly

Learning Labels

* singing in unison

* memorising a melody

* choosing and performing actions to a steady beat

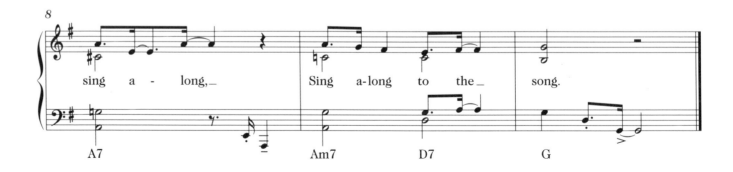